COMTE AND THE METAPHYSICIANS,

IN REPLY TO AN ARTICLE

ON

POSITIVISM,

IN

THE EDINBURGH REVIEW, APRIL, 1866.

~~~~~~~~~~~~~~~~~~~~~~~~~~~~~~~~~~~~

BY

A POSITIVIST.

Calcutta:

PRINTED BY I. C. BOSE & CO., STANHOPE PRESS, 172, BOW-BAZAR ROAD.

1868.

COMTE AND THE METAPHYSICIANS.

In the *Edinburgh Review* for April 1868, there appeared a very full and able account of Comte's life and system. The writer of the article appears to accept so much that it is difficult to see why he does not accept still more, and certainly the principles he is willing to concede, involve important conclusions which he does not hesitate to reject. He is of opinion that Comte's "undoubted influence lies in certain great conceptions, with which he has enriched and illuminated the modern mind." He then proceeds to review and criticise these conceptions, and from the terms employed it would appear that he accepts (1) the *positive method* entirely ; (2) the *classification of the sciences*, except so far as it relates to man himself ; and (3) the *sociological doctrine* to a certain extent, and as we believe to an extent which involves the complete downfal of the metaphysical philosophy. Allowing thus much an attempt is yet made to show that there is a science which is more than science, that there is a region of the invisible, about which, although all the requisites of knowledge are wanting, certain definite information can be obtained, that metaphysics in fact are not concerned with discussions which are fruitless and illusory.

I.—As regards the Positive method, the Reviewer observes as follows :—" The Positive method is the basis of the Positive philosophy, and it is peculiarly necessary to distinguish it from this philosophy, because there is a sense in which the method is universally accredited and accepted. What is this method ? It is nothing more nor less than the application of the principle that in the study of nature we are concerned merely *with the facts before us and the relations* which connect these facts with one another. We have nothing to do with the supposed essence or hidden nature of the facts. Their absolute character, cause, or purpose, is beyond our scrutiny. The science of any order of phenomena has nothing to do with the origin or ultimate explanation of the phenomena, but simply with their observed properties and the laws or order of sequence, according to which these properties are formed and subsist. *Facts, and the invariable laws which govern them*, are, in other words, the pursuit, and the only legitimate pursuit of science. This is the method of Positive enquiry now universally recognised in every department of science, although as yet imperfectly carried out in some."

The Reviewer then observes justly that Comte was not and did not claim to be the originator of this method, but that he is entitled to "great merit for the luminous consistency with which he has applied it to all natural phenomena, and so expelled from the domain of science many original and mystical hypotheses, which lingered in his time, and even still linger." "Comte did well in expelling all such hypotheses from the scientific domain. He has at once given it (the positive method) a wider application than any previous thinker, and far more clearly understood its import." Although allowing thus much the Reviewer will not admit the illusory nature of all metaphysical enquiries. He, in fact, regards science as two-fold, namely, science proper which is concerned with phenomena alone, and science metaphysical which is concerned apparently with the ideas which the mind introduces when dealing with phenomena, ideas which compel us, according to the Reviewer, to postulate a Creator, a Supreme Intelligent Will, a Divine purpose, a region of the Invisible. The principal argument employed to sustain this view is that science works with certain conceptions which are not found in the phenomena but are the contributions of the mind itself. Such for example are our conceptions of Law, Force, and Cause—"rational concepts which no mere observation of phenomena can yield." We imagine that there is nothing in the reasoning employed in this part of the discussion with which a Comtist might not agree, in fact no one has insisted more strongly than Comte himself upon the compound nature of all our knowledge, into which both a subjective and an objective element must always enter. Speaking of the maxim '*there is nothing in the understanding that did not originally spring from sensation*,' Comte observes, "The moderns often pressed this axiom too far. They represented our intelligence as purely passive. This compelled Leibnitz to add an essential restriction. The object of that restriction was, definitely to express the spontaneous character of our mental dispositions. Leibnitz's addition, *except the understanding*, was completed by Kant. Kant introduced the distinction never to be forgotten, between objective and subjective reality, both equally applicable to all man's conceptions." Again, when characterising the order of the universe, Comte says, "this order is at once *objective* and *subjec-*

tive; in other words it concerns equally the *object* contemplated and the *subject* which contemplates. Physical laws in fact imply logical laws, and *vice versa.*" Thus it will be seen that Comte does not in any way deny that in order to reach a law there must be a distinct mental contribution to the phenomena before us; that he fully admits that we do bring to the interpretation of the facts "a light beyond what we get from them—a rational element which is not the product of any mere sense-experience." But he does maintain, what perhaps the Reviewer would not allow, that the subjective is intimately dependent on the objective element, and that the former cannot function without the latter. "With regard to our highest spiritual functions" says Comte, "equally as with regard to our most corporeal ones, the external world serves us for nourishment, stimulus, and control." Confining ourselves, however, to the actual statements of the Reviewer, we cannot see that the mere assumption of a strictly mental element which transforms the products of sense into products of the understanding, entitles him to conclude that "the root of science is something more than science," that "the physical finds its explanation, its intelligibility, only through the metaphysical." Surely this is a strange use of the term 'metaphysical,' to make it apply to those ordinary conceptions which the mind contributes to the isolated phenomena of nature, those ideal bonds by means of which we colligate the facts which sense offers to intelligence. When Comte branded as fruitless all metaphysical enquiries, he had in view not the results of reason itself but problems which the experience of ages has shown to be insoluble, problems which relate to the *hidden* essences of things, the origin and purpose of the world, the plan of creation, the designs and workings of Omnipotence; problems which transcend reason, and which accordingly involve those who attempt to solve them in the most inextricable confusion.

The very mode in which the Reviewer works out his thesis appears to us to be a striking evidence of the perplexity in which we are involved, immediately we attempt to trespass beyond the boundaries of the visible and intelligible world.

Having first informed his readers that Law and Order do not belong to the phenomena themselves, but are super-imposed upon them by the mind of man, he afterwards speaks of the Supreme Will going forth incessantly among natural laws, and using them as instruments for its purpose. Where then, let us ask, are these natural laws among which the Divine wanders as of old He walked among the groves and bosky dells of Eden? Are they in the mind of man, or in the world without? If in the mind of man, surely the language employed about the Supreme Will is quite inapplicable; and if both in the mind and in the world without, then the idea of law is not necessarily super-imposed by the mind upon the cosmical phenomena which surround it.

The process by which we are supposed to arrive at the knowledge of an All-wise Being, appears to be a complicated one, and very different from the instinctive belief of our forefathers to whom this Being had revealed himself as the Righteous Judge, the All-powerful King, the Ever-present Friend who delivereth his chosen from all their troubles, the Lord who conversed with Adam in the garden, and spake with Moses, face to face, upon the slopes of Sinai,—thus appearing to them not as a mere ~~attribute~~ *substratum* of Force, or as the slave of Law, but as the Living God whose Will is unrestrained, whose action is free, who causeth the vapours to ascend from the ends of the earth, who maketh lightnings with rain, and who bringeth forth the wind out of his treasures—how unlike is such a Being to the poor metaphysical entity, the attenuated abstraction of the ontologist. According to the Edinburgh Reviewer man thus arrives at his conception of the Deity.—" Neither Law nor Force, in any simple form, is adequate to explain any class of phenomena, illuminating as it is to the mind to be able to gather up its knowledge in such ultimate ratios as the law of gravitation. We still keep asking What is the Force? Why is the Law? We must get beneath even such ultimate conceptions as these, and lay hold of the living power of mind of which they are merely the attributes or expression. It is only by adding our mind to nature that we can reach these conceptions; and so it is only by carrying them out into their full meaning that we find any real explanation in them as applied to nature. When we penetrate behind Law to the reason which speaks in it—when we recognise in force the Will whose attribute it is—then, and not till then, do we approach a solution of the phenomena in which we can rest and find satisfaction. And therefore, as formerly we emerged upon the metaphysical sphere in the mere attempt to vindicate the language of science, so now we emerge upon the theological in the attempt to read the full meaning of this language as applied to nature. Law and Force are nothing in nature; if they do not bespeak an intelligent Power governing and sustaining it. They explain nothing except in so far as they denote such a Power."

There is an appearance of contradiction in this language, inasmuch as Law and Force seem here to be regarded as inherent in phenomena, whereas it was before maintained that they were conceptions contributed by the mind and not to be found in nature. Unless this contradiction is cleared up, it is impossible to make the arguments employed consistent with each other. If Law is a purely mental conception, then surely we need not go further than the mind itself for an explanation of it; but if Law, either simple or complex, is inherent in external phenomena, then there can be no need for us to supply it to nature, and it does not exist simply because we cannot conceive phenomena except as existing under the conditions which it implies. Taking, however, Law and Force to be purely mental conceptions, they no doubt bespeak the power of man in whom they reside, but it is difficult to see, at least to us, how they bespeak the Intelligent Power of any other Being. If we ask why man colligates facts by laws, and animates brute matter with force, the simple answer is that he does so in obedience to the necessities of his own constitution, and that for anything we know to the contrary his doing so may be quite as much a sign of impotence as of infallible wisdom. When we speak of the Creator, as an Intelligent Power, the Supreme Will, and so forth, we are but shaping for ourselves an Idol, clothed with human attributes, spiritual it may be but human nevertheless. The metaphysician, to use the expressive language of a contemporary divine,* "strips off from humanity just so much as suits his purpose;—'and the residue thereof he maketh a God';—less pious in his idolatry than the carver of the graven image, in that he does not fall down to it and pray unto it, but is content to stand afar off and reason concerning it. * * * Surely downright idolatry is better than this *rational* worship of a fragment of humanity. * * * Better to realise the satire of the Eleatic philosopher, to make God in the likeness of man, even as the ox or the horse might conceive gods in the form of oxen or horses, than to adore some half-hewn Hermes, the head of a man joined to a misshapen block."

The Reviewer objects to the language of Comte when he says that "Theological philosophy supposes every thing to be governed by Will, and that phenomena are consequently variable and irregular." Such a statement embodies, accord-

* Rev. H. L. Mansel, D. D. See Bampton Lectures for 1858; Lecture I. p. 12, (4th edition.)

ing to the Reviewer, a crude and ignorant conception. "Theology" he maintains, "knows nothing of a conflict between order and will. * * * The Divine Will is the type of all Law and order. If there is a Divine Will at all, it must be a Will acting by general laws, by methods, of which order is an invariable characteristic; and the presence of order or law, through all the domain of nature, is exactly what the enlightened Theist would expect. If anywhere he came upon disorder, instead of order, chaos instead of a cosmos—instead of finding any satisfaction in the idea of supernatural Will, he would loose hold of this idea altogether. It would vanish with its sign. The question is not one of Will *versus* Order, at least with the Theist, but of Will *plus* Order, Intelligence *plus* Law." Now with regard to the position here adopted, we have only to observe that the term Will is used in a purely technical and special acceptation, and not in the ordinary theological sense of a faculty homogeneous with the corresponding faculty in man, free and propitiable, so that its action will not allow, at all events, of *scientific* prevision. If, as the Reviewer maintains, the idea of a Divine Will is chained, as it were, to the idea of Order—the Divine Will being the type of Law and Order, while Order is the sign of the Divine Will,—then the terms are simply convertible, the distinction between them vanishing into a mere verbal difference. If it be true that the theological conception grows more perfect as the reign of law is found to be more and more extensive, then it must be most perfect when law is universal, in which case the Divine action must be exercised within certain prescribed limits, and the word Omnipotence becomes a misnomer. The term, however, as employed by the Reviewer, has really no intelligible meaning. Will is an essentially human attribute, which, owing to its supposed freedom, appears to confer upon man an independent power of initiation, and hence has always been transferred from man himself to the objects of his worship, whether animate or inanimate, natural or supernatural. Take away this freedom, make Will but the simple concomitant of Law, and the principal notions of Theology are at once emptied of their meaning. Sin, Sacrifice, Prayer, Thanksgiving become mere words, or else the symbols of artifices which may be usefully retained for regulative purposes, but which cannot impose upon the enlightened metaphysician whose God merely registers the decrees of a Deity more powerful than himself—the omnipotent and inexorable Kosmos.

The Reviewer seems to imagine that a rational conception of the universe necessarily leads us to the conclusion that the universe itself is the production of Mind. Now as the mind which contemplates is a part of the universe, this conclusion would involve the position, that Mind created mind, or that, in other words, the Creator made man in his own image, thus bringing us round to the old theological doctrine which is essentially anthropomorphic. Take almost any metaphysical dogma in the same way and try to give it a meaning, you will find in the end that it receives whatever logical consistency it may possess from some fragment of humanity which it has distorted and disguised.

The Purpose which we find in nature is, as the Reviewer allows, derived from the light thrown upon it by our own reason: apart from mind the most curious are equally dumb with the most familiar phenomena of the external world. But this idea of Purpose being derived from our own minds, why are we to regard it as any thing more than a convenient fiction, a regulative artifice? Why conclude that the measure of our own weakness is the standard of Omnipotence, and that the great I Am must work under the same limitations which have been imposed upon us, the creatures of a day? Pure Theology does not contemplate that marked division between the realms of the natural and supernatural, between the spiritual and material man, on which the metaphysical philosophy so strongly insists. The positive, as distinguished from the metaphysical, theologian regards the supernatural order as the prevailing one; with him the natural is not fixed but is constantly liable to be disturbed by the supernatural; with him the object of adoration is a living, personal God, and not an abstract essence, the source of that real being which is hidden "behind the veil;" with him the soul is not a separate entity belonging to the realm of the incognoscible, a spiritual existence devoid of almost every attribute of humanity, but a true image of the individual, a vivid effigy of which the body is merely the gross envelope, and which at the hour of death escapes from its prison-house, a living person endowed with human form and sense and intelligence—man in the nature of its attributes, more than man only in the increased perfection of those attributes.

II.—As regards Comte's classification of the sciences, the Reviewer observes, " there is no one capable of appreciating the task who will be disposed to undervalue what he has done in this respect. Others may, to some extent, have anticipated him; but no one who has really mastered his system of classification, the principles on which it is based, and the rich and frequently striking thoughts with which he has expounded its sequences, can entertain any question of his ability and originality as a scientific thinker." Again when speaking of the principle of classification, he says, " In seeking for a principle on which to co-ordinate the series of abstract sciences, Comte has recourse to the simple idea of arranging them according to their respective generality and the degree of dependence which they bear to one another. The idea is simple enough, and it is absurd to claim any particular credit for it; but it is at least as absurd to cast any ridicule or discredit upon it. To begin with the most general or elementary branches . and advance to the more complex and difficult—what is this, some have said, but to follow the instinct of all sensible people—what ninety-nine people out of a hundred would do? But the plain answer to this is that, not to speak of the ninety-nine, not even the hundredth philosopher had succeeded in exhibiting the physical sciences in a rational series before Comte. The simplicity of the idea upon which he worked, which guided his great faculty of co-ordination, does not detract from, but rather enhances, the merit of the scheme." And yet, strange to say, though thoroughly appreciating the gigantic task which was accomplished by Comte, though accepting his principle of classification, and believing that it applies to the following sciences, mathematics, astronomy, physics, chemistry, and physiology—the Reviewer would nevertheless reject 'the crowning services' which Comte has rendered to thought, namely, the elaboration of a positive science of mind upon the basis of Gall's preliminary attempt, and also the construction of a theory of society consistent with the facts of history and the nature of the individual man.

In man, according to the Reviewer, there are two orders of being, the spiritual and the natural, which are heterogeneous, so that the study of mind does not pre-suppose that of matter, but rests upon a basis of its own and demands a method different from that which is employed in the physical sciences. Bound by his principles to recognise only physical phenomena, Comte, says the Reviewer, "pushes his objective method beyond its proper stretch, and it crumbles in his hands." Now with respect to that whole school of thinkers which willingly accepts Comte's classification up to a certain point,—that is so long as it does not necessarily run counter to their precouceived metaphysical theories—we cannot but regard the members of this school as open to the charge of strange inconsistency. They lavish upon Comte excessive praise for ' his great force of intellect, his marvellous genius for scientific method, his powerful faculty of co-ordinating knowledge, his luminous insight into the true meaning of scientific ideas, and their fruitful relations to one another'; they accept his positive method, his classification of the *physical* sciences, and much of his sociological doctrine; they admit the fundamental principles, and yet refuse to allow that the great master-mind which gave birth to them was the best judge of the inevitable consequences to which they must lead. Surely if Comte's intellect was so vast, and his power of execution so wonderful as these adversaries allow, he could not have failed to perceive that the statue he had hewn from the unformed marble with such prodigious labour was but a beautiful torso which still wanted the head to render it the image of the perfect man. Comte never was aware of any such deficiency, but, on the contrary, always regarded his work as forming one indissoluble whole, that which his metaphysico-scientific admirers accept being with him merely the indispensable foundation upon which the other portion, which he regarded as the actual edifice, rested. For our part, we feel more confidence in the bold and uncompromising language of Comte, than in the timid and distracted counsels of his almost reluctant adversaries—in the conflict of opinion which is now raging who can doubt that victory will, in the end, attend upon the leader whose forces are most united, whose plan of action is most intelligible ?

The so-called science of psychology has been omitted by Comte, because, so far as it is positive, it is included under Biology and Morals; the metaphysical portion of course must be discarded from a system which proclaims all metaphysical researches to be fruitless and delusive ; while that internal observation which has hitherto been the only organ of discovery upon which the majority of positive Psychologists have relied, has proved to be too untrustworthy an instrument to entitle it to claim any great consideration from those who wield the more trenchant weapons furnished by the purely physical sciences. The distinction between mind and matter so much insisted upon by metaphysicians seems to us an idle one : it is not essential to theology, for Christianity dispensed with it by proclaiming the dogma of the resurrection of the body. The distinction proceeds simply from a desire to confer a fictitious dignity upon one part of man's nature at the expense of the rest, and this object it attains not by constituting a hierarchy of functions, but by forcibly separating mind from the body and its environment, and by carving out for it an imaginary empire over which it should bear unlimited sway. Moreover the metaphysical doctrine appears to us untenable because it errs against that fundamental principle of logic which bids us always form the simplest hypothesis consistent with all the ascertained data. That mind is a function of a certain organism is an assumption at once simple and fruitful in its consequences, while the rival hypothesis is not only complex but altogether barren of results. The value of the so-called subjective method in mental science has been well estimated by Dr. Maudsley, who, as being one of the most eminent physicians of the present day, speaks with an authority which cannot fail to command respect.

" Plainly" he says " it is not possible by simple observation of others to form true inductions as to their mental phenomena ; the defect of an observation which reaches only to the visible results of invisible operations, exposes us without protection to the hypocrisy, conscious or unconscious, of the individual ; and the positive tendency, which no one can avoid, to interpret the action of another mind according to the measure of one's own, to see not what is in the object, but what is in the subject, frequently vitiates an assumed penetration into motives. If we call to our aid the principles of the received system of psychology, matters are not mended ; for its ill-defined terms and vague traditions, injuriously affecting our perceptions, and over-ruling our understanding, do not fail to confuse and falsify inferences. It must unfortunately be added that, in the present state of physiological science, it is quite impossible to ascertain, by observation and experiment, the nature of those organic processes which are the bodily conditions of mental phenomena. There would appear, then, to be no help for it but to have entire recourse to the psychological method—that method of interrogating self-consciousness which has found so much favor at all times. * * * The method of interrogating self-consciousness may be employed, and is largely employed, without carrying it to a metaphysical extreme. Empirical psychology, founded on *direct* consciousness as distinguished from the *transcendental* consciousness on which metaphysics is based, claims to give a faithful record of our different states of mind and their mutual relations, and has been extravagantly lauded by the Scotch school, as an inductive science. Its value as a science must plainly rest upon the sufficiency and reliability of consciousness as a witness of that which takes place in the mind. Is the foundation then sufficiently secure ? It may well be doubted ; and for the following reasons :—

(*a*.) There are but few individuals who are capable of attending to the succession of phenomena in their own minds; such introspection demanding a particular cultivation, and being practised with success by those only who have learned the terms, and been imbued with the theories, of the system of psychology supposed to be thereby established.

(*b*.) There is no agreement between those who have acquired the power of introspection : and men of apparently equal cultivation and capacity will, with the utmost sincerity and confidence, lay down directly contradictory propositions. It is not possible to convince either opponent of error, as it might be in a matter of objective science, because he appeals to a witness whose evidence can be taken by no one but himself, and whose veracity, therefore, cannot be tested.

(*c*.) To direct consciousness inwardly to the observation of a particular state of mind, is to isolate that activity for the time, to cut it off from its relations, and, therefore, to render it unnatural. In order to observe its own action, it is necessary that the mind pause from activity ; and yet it is the train of activity that is to be observed. As long as you cannot effect the pause necessary for self-contemplation, there can be no observation of the current of activity : if the pause is effected, then there can be nothing to observe. This cannot be accounted a vain and theoretical objection ; for the results of introspection too surely confirm its validity : what was a question once is a question still, and instead of being resolved by introspective analysis is only fixed and fed.

(*d*.) The madman's delusion is of itself sufficient to excite profound distrust, not only in the objective truth, but in the subjective worth of the testimony of an individual's self-consciousness. Descartes laid it down as the fundamental proposition of philosophy that whatever the mind could clearly and distinctly conceive, was true : if there is one thing more clearly and distinctly conceived than another, it is commonly the madman's delusion. No marvel, then, that psychologists, since the time of Descartes, have held that the veracity of consciousness is to be relied upon only under certain rules from the violation of which, Sir W. Hamilton believed, the contradictions of philosophy have arisen. On what evidence then do the rules rest ? Either on the evidence of consciousness, whence it happens that each philosopher and each lunatic has his own rules, and no advance is made ; or upon the observation and judgment of mankind, to confess which is very much like throwing self-consciousness overboard—not otherwise than as was advantageously done by positive science when the figures on the thermometer, and not the subjective feelings of heat or cold, were recognised to be the true test of the individual's temperature."

III. Speaking of Comte's sociology, the Reviewer says, " its success will be estimated differently according to our point of view, there are few even of those most strongly repudiating Comte's principles who would deny the great and just conception that underlies his sociological scheme. Other thinkers before him had conceived of human society as regulated by natural laws, and so presenting throughout its course a great law of development. * * * But however this idea may have dawned upon other thinkers, none before had evolved it so fully or worked it out so thoroughly as a scientific conception. Here, as in the preceding department of science, it is Comte's great merit that he has applied the Positive conception without reserve, and shown that looking *merely at the phenomena of* society, no less than at the phenomena of life and the phenomena of physical action, they present an invariable order, facts following facts in rigorous sequence. That Politics is a science in short, and that law reigns there as supreme as in other departments of human knowledge, are truths, the growing diffusion of which is very much owing to the Positive Philosophy.

" And not only so, Comte has not only established the scientific character of social phenomena in a more perfect manner than any previous philosopher, but he has also established their *distinctive* scientific character. He has brought out the essential bearing of history upon politics, and shown how all the phenomena of human society are what they are, not merely as the result of human nature *per se*, but as the result of *historical human nature.* History is not merely a sequence linking age to age by inevitable laws of progress, but society, at every particular stage of its progress, bears the impress of all that has gone before, and social phenomena are in consequence a historical deposit, and not merely a result of individual human life. Man, in short, as a social being, yields a definite science, because there goes to his making not merely the radical propensities which the study of the individual man reveals, but all the special conditions arising out of the sequency of events in the midst of which he stands.

" So far we join with Comte's admirers in conceding the great merit of his sociological conception. We agree with Mr. Mill that it is impossible for any political thinker to claim a hearing who has not mastered this conception and recognised the essential relation of historical studies to social and political speculation."

And yet though admitting all this, the Reviewer, it would appear, refuses to accept the fundamental law upon which the social theory of Positivism is based. This law is evidently rejected because its acceptance would involve the admission that both theology and metaphysics are transitory, and deal with problems which experience has shown to be insoluble. But this law, as the Reviewer justly observes, " underlies not only Comte's general conception of philosophy, but constitutes its special sociological doctrine." It is in fact so inwoven with the whole texture of the Positive system, that it cannot be removed without essential injury to the substance of which it forms a part. Those who reject this law and also the application of the Positive method to the mind of man, reject just so much as is at variance with their pre-conceived theories; but, unfortunately, what they throw aside with such profound contempt, is the very basis of the whole fabric, the keystone of the arch, that without which the edifice lacks unity of design and is devoid of any useful object.

The controversy between the disciples and adversaries of Comte may indeed be reduced to this single issue :—Is the law of the three stages true, or is it false? If true, then theology and metaphysics are doomed, and the triumph of a doctrine of Humanity is but the work of time. We believe that that law is true, and that one of the best confirmations of it arises from the hopeless confusion in which men are and ever have been involved directly they quit the region of experience to embark on the dark and limitless ocean of metaphysical speculation. Let the question by all means be narrowed, as the Reviewer wishes, to the essential idea or mode of conception, out of which the law of the three stages as well as all the special doctrine of Positivism spring. We have no fear as to the result, and we are confident that the day is not far distant when the positive mode of thought will be universal, while the metaphysical, if it exists at all, will linger, like astrology and alchemy, merely among minds of an exceptional order. One of the most prominent characteristics of the present day, according to an acute observer* " is the little favour in which metaphysics is held, and the very general conviction that there is no profit in it : the consequence of which firmly fixed belief is, that it is cultivated as a science only by those whose particular business it is to do so, who are engaged not in action, wherein the true balance of life is maintained, but in dreaming in professional chairs ; or, if by any others, by the ambitious youth who goes through an attack of metaphysics as a child goes through an attack of measles, getting haply an immunity from a similar affection for the rest of his life ; or lastly, by the untrained and immature intellects of those metaphysical dabblers who continue youths for life." The whole energy of Comte's commanding intellect, the whole artillery of his vast knowledge were directed towards the demolition of the metaphysical philosophy, and if he did not succeed in discrediting the system which he attacked, it may be safely asserted that he has done nothing worthy of extraordinary praise. Merely to classify the physical sciences according to their order of development, and to discern that human progress followed *some* law *or other*, are not tasks that required the genius of a Comte to accomplish, nor when accomplished were they likely to confer any signal benefit upon the human race. Comte's object was a far higher one than simply to erect another temple to science : it was to destroy completely the metaphysical system which was stopping the path of human progress, and to build upon its ruins a new philosophy which should succeed in gaining the consensus of western nations in the same or even in a higher degree than Catholicism had succeeded, and which should offer a doctrine fitted to gain, in course of time, *universal* acceptance. In the noble edifice which Comte erected, the classification of the physical sciences, and the simple conception that human society is regulated by natural laws, were essential parts it is true, but they were only parts and were kept strictly subordinate to the general plan and to the ultimate object which the whole was designed to secure.

---

* Dr. Maudsley's ' Physiology and Pathology of the Mind,' p. 8.

The Reviewer seems to be surprised that Mr. Lewes should place the law of the three stages upon the same level with the law of gravitation. To those who reject Comte's great law of development, its importance of course is nil; but to those who, like Mr. Lewes, believe in this law and regard it as furnishing the clue to man's history, its importance cannot be otherwise than overwhelming. To the simple-minded adherents of Comte, it *is* quite as true "that the theological and metaphysical are merely passing phases of society towards the positive or final stage from which all ideas of a higher divine order are banished, as that the heavens move in an undeviating order, the proportions of which are expressed in the formula 'directly as the mass and inversely as the square of the distance.'" To these credulous votaries of an absurd faith, the law of the three stages rivals in its truth but far surpasses in its importance the law of gravitation.

The only evidence that we have in favor of any natural law is the coincidence between the results deduced from the law, and the actual results as given by observation. This is the evidence on which we accept the laws of motion, and therefore also the law of gravitation which depends upon them, and similar evidence must verify the law of the three stages in order that it may be classed among the fundamental principles of positive science. Now we believe that Comte has furnished us with exactly the amount and kind of evidence that is required, and accordingly that his great law of sociology is entitled to rank with the universally admitted laws of physics, chemistry, and biology.

In conclusion we would observe that the article we have been noticing is, in the main, extremely fair; it is, therefore, to be regretted that the writer of it should occasionally have allowed the partisan to usurp the place of the judge. As an instance of what we mean, the note at p. 350 may be adduced, in which a contrast is drawn between the religion of humanity and the religion of the gospel—a contrast, as may be expected, unfavorable to the former. Commenting upon the contemptuous terms in which Comte's speaks of many human beings, as 'born upon the earth merely to manure it,' 'mere digesting machines' 'forming no real part of humanity' the Reviewer exclaims :—"Here the essential exclusiveness of all merely human religion comes out—how different from the human ideal of the Gospel, which is 'preached to the poor', and which came 'to save that which was lost'! The Reviewer, when he penned these lines, must surely have forgotten that Christianity condemns to everlasting perdition all but an insignificant fragment of the human race. The world in general, we imagine, would regard that dispensation which sentenced the reprobate merely to manure the earth, as a kinder one than that which assigned them to the eternal torments of hell-fire.

I. C. Bose & Co., 172, Bow Bazar Road, Calcutta.

www.ingramcontent.com/pod-product-compliance
Lightning Source LLC
Chambersburg PA
CBHW082058070426
42452CB00052B/2736